From God to You

Scott Curran

To you -- my friend in God.

Contents

Introduction

From God to You is a book of contemplation. It's written from the point of view of God speaking to you. It includes reflections on scripture and paraphrases of scripture. If you'd like to use the book for daily reflections, it's divided into thirty chapters, one for each day of the month. Peace be with you, my spiritual friend.

Chapter 1 - Genesis to Job

I made you. I made everything, and it's all good.

Avoid notions of duality.

All is one in me.

Wherever you are, I'm there.

Everything that happens is ordained by me.

Everything you experience is part of a higher purpose.

If others harm you, I make good come from it. So don't retaliate against those who hurt you. Put them at ease and be kind to them.

I'm above, below, within and all around.

The place where you're standing is holy ground.

My presence goes with you.

There's nothing to worry about.

I'm with you wherever you go.

I turn your darkness into light.

Can you make a tree? Can you make a galaxy?

I'm the creator and sustainer of the universe and of you.

Do you think I need you to tell me what to do?

Sometimes you wonder, 'Why this? Why now?' What difference does it make? I didn't make a mistake.

Everything's the way it's meant to be.

Genesis 1:31 Genesis 2:17 Genesis 28:16 Genesis 50:20-21
Exodus 3:5 Exodus 33:14 Joshua 1:9 2 Samuel 22:29 Job
40:1-2 Job 40:2

.

Chapter 2 - Psalms Part 1

I fill your heart with joy and set you free.

In me, you look at everything differently.

I'm your refuge.

I guide and provide.

Being aware of my presence, nothing shakes you.

I'm the Life of your Life.

Everything's perfect just the way it is.

I give you everything you need.

I guide you to green pastures.

I bring you to peaceful waters.

I restore your soul and make you whole.

Even in the deepest darkness, I'm with you.

I protect you and comfort you.

I bless you in a myriad of ways.

I'm with you all of your days.

Your home is in heaven.

I trim self-will away.

I show you my way.

I'm your light and your salvation.

In me, you see clearly.

I lift you out of the depths.

When you call for help, I heal you.

When you're heading for spiritual death, I save you.

I bring you through a night of tears into the light of a new day.

You've acknowledged your sins, and you've been forgiven.

When you're broken-hearted, I console you.

When you're crushed in spirit, I restore you.

I'm the source and essence of all that is.

In my light, you see light.

Psalm 4:7 Psalm 9:9 Psalm 16:5 Psalm 16:8 Psalm 16:11 Psalm 18:30 Psalm 23 Psalm 25:8-9 Psalm 27:1 Psalm 30:1-5 Psalm 32:5 Psalm 34:18-19 Psalm 36:9

Chapter 3 - Psalms Part 2

Let others live the way they choose to live. Leave them to me.

Live in the awareness of my love and mercy.

My light is shining through you. It's brighter than the sun.

My love is flowing through you -- and touching everyone.

Trust in me. Act with love.

Delight in me.

Whatever happens is my will and whatever I will is what's best for you.

Your awareness of my presence affects not only you, but everyone around you too.

Be gentle and humble.

In me, you have peace.

Your earthly life is short. From a spiritual perspective, it's briefer than a breath.

Desire only that things be the way they are and that things happen the way they happen. You'll always be content.

Relax in the awareness of me.

I'm creating a pure heart in you.

I'm putting a new and trusting spirit in you.

I'm transforming you.

Leave things to me. I'm taking care of everything.

Only in me do you find serenity.

You can't be satisfied by what's temporary. You find peace in me alone.

I'm with you always, even when it seems like the darkness is your only friend.

Don't take things too seriously.

See, in everything, the unfolding of the Divine mystery.

Psalm 37:1-11 Psalm 39:5 Psalm 40:4 Psalm 46:10 Psalm 51:10 Psalm 55:22 Psalm 62:1-7 Psalm 88:18 Psalm 94:18-19

Chapter 4 - Psalms Part 3

I redeem your life from the pit.

I bless you with kindness and mercy.

I don't treat you as your sins deserve.

I don't repay you according to your wrongs.

As high as the sky goes up from the earth, so great is my love for you.

As far as the East is from the West, so far have I removed your sins from you.

Your earthly life is like a wildflower. It flourishes for a while in a field. Then the wind blows and it's gone. Before long, no one remembers it was there.

My love is eternal.

In your anguish, cry out to me.

I set you free.

Only in me do you find peace.

Don't be dismayed when others hurt you or disappoint you. You hurt and disappoint others too.

The feelings and opinions of humans fluctuate, but I remain constant.

It's better to trust in me than to depend on people.

I made this day. Enjoy it!

Fill your heart with a joyful song.

Be thankful for everything, no matter what's going on.

All that happens is meant to be.

Everything's designed to bring you to me.

I created your inmost being.

I formed you in your mother's womb.

Consider what an amazing creation you are!

You're wonderfully made!

You were conceived in my mind long before you were conceived in human form. I knew you before you were born!

I decided when you'd arrive on earth. I decided when and where your mother would give birth.

One day you'll leave your physical body behind. I know the exact place and time.

Every moment of your life has been ordained by me, and I love you -- unconditionally.

Psalm 103:10-16 Psalm 118 Psalm 136:1 Psalm 139:13-16

Chapter 5 - Proverbs

Trust me with all your heart.

Don't rely on what you think you know.

Most of your talking is useless chatter about things that don't matter. Be quiet.

Don't deride anyone.

Be generous -- with money, with mercy and with acts of kindness.

When you help others feel better, you feel better too.

Overlook insults.

I work in my perfect way with everybody.

Leave yourself and others to me.

Let go and let me. 'Live and let live.'

Trusting in me makes you joyful and peaceful.

Stay calm. Use words with restraint.

Be honest and transparent.

Be as bold as a lion.

Proverbs 3:5-6 Proverbs 10:19 Proverbs 11:12 Proverbs 11:25 Proverbs 12:16 Proverbs 16:20 Proverbs 17:27 Proverbs 28:1

Chapter 6 - Ecclesiastes and Wisdom

There's a time for everything.

I've placed you in your current circumstances for a purpose.

My will is revealed in the events of each moment.

You're exactly where you're supposed to be.

I fill the whole world and hold everything together.

I created everything, and everything I created is wholesome and good.

I'm merciful. I overlook sin. I transform you from within.

I love every living being.

My imperishable spirit is in everything.

Ecclesiastes 3:1 Wisdom 1:7 Wisdom 1:14 Wisdom 11:23
Wisdom 11:27 Wisdom 12:1

Chapter 7 - Sirach

All wisdom comes from me.

I'm looking after you.

If you're humiliated, be patient.

Trust in my Divine Providence.

Accept, with gratitude, whatever is, and whatever happens.

With loving, reverential awe of me, live in humility.

Look forward to ever more blessings and eternal happiness.

I help you in times of trouble.

I'm merciful and kind.

I've forgiven your sins.

I've given you a peaceful mind.

Your destiny is in my hands, not in human hands.

My mercy is as great as my majesty.

Humiliation, thwarted desires, loneliness and shame; Rejection, obscurity, suffering and pain: Experiencing such things helps you to eradicate your pride. It is through the humble that I'm glorified.

The more humble you are, the more you glorify me.

Pride begins when you forget about me.

Pride imprisons you. Humility sets you free.

Have a healthy self respect, infused with humility.

Remember who you are in me.

Everything comes from me, whatever it may be: life and death, failure and success, wealth and poverty.

Accept everything with equanimity.

Turn to me, and experience the magnitude of my mercy.

I have compassion for every living being.

Sirach 1:1   Sirach 2:2-18   Sirach 3:20   Sirach 10:12-13
Sirach 10:28 Sirach 11:14 Sirach 17:29 Sirach 18:13

Chapter 8 - Isaiah

The whole earth is full of my glory.

I'm your creator and your savior.

I give you power and strength.

In me, you deal well with everything.

Keep your mind on me and trust me, and I'll keep you in perfect peace.

I'm holding your hand. Everything's okay. I'm helping you.

Forget the past. In me, everything's new and everything's now.

I'm ahead of you and behind.

My thoughts aren't like your thoughts. My ways aren't like your ways. As the heavens are higher than the earth, so are my thoughts and ways higher than yours.

Go out in joy and peace.

The mountains and hills will greet you with a happy song, and all the trees will clap their hands.

I'm the potter. You're the clay.

I'm bringing you to perfection in my own way.

You're my creation and I'm fashioning you. Leave it to me, and be at peace.

Isaiah 6:3 Isaiah 12:2 Isaiah 26:3 Isaiah 41:13 Isaiah 43:18
Isaiah 52:12 Isaiah 55:8-12 Isaiah 64:8

Chapter 9 - Jeremiah to Zechariah

Your life isn't yours.

Apart from me, you're nothing, and you can do nothing.

I'm the Life of your Life.

You don't control things. I do.

Whatever is and whatever occurs is what's best for you.

Would you like to be peaceful? Would you like to be free? Then get rid of your notions of how things should be. Abandon your will and your life to me.

I fill heaven and earth.

I'm in every atom and in every cell. I'm throughout the universe as well. I'm everywhere.

I love you with a constant and everlasting love.

My love doesn't fluctuate based on your achievements or your shortcomings. It's unconditional.

In the awareness of your oneness with me, wonderful and amazing things are revealed to you.

Look at everything in a new way.

You accomplish things and overcome things not by your own strength or willpower, but by my spirit.

Turn everything over to me.

Jeremiah 10:23-24 Jeremiah 31:3 Jeremiah 33:3 Zechariah 4:6

Chapter 10 - Matthew Part 1

Joseph, the husband of Mary, is a model of humility, strength, kindness, wisdom and faith.

In the desert, you discover deeper levels of love and humility. Angels are with you.

Being poor in spirit is knowing that, apart from me, you're nothing.

I'm the only thing that's real.

In me, you have everything. You're in the kingdom of heaven.

You're blessed when you're merciful.

I love you, even though you're not as loving as you'd like to be.

I understand the shortcomings that are part of your humanity.

Surrender yourself to me. Be a channel of my mercy.

You are the light of the world. I'm not saying that you could be, that you were or that you will be. I'm saying that you are the light of the world.

In me, you're a transparency, revealing Love.

You're the light of the world because I'm the light of the world and I'm within you.

Don't hide the light. Let it shine. It's not your light. It's mine.

If someone strikes you on one cheek, turn to them the other also.

Love your enemies. Pray for those who persecute you.

When you pray, don't do it for show. Don't babble on or talk fancy. I know what you need.

My will is done on earth as it is in heaven. It's made manifest within you and around you.

Unite your will with mine in prayer.

In my peace, you see peace everywhere.

Don't worry about your life.

I provide -- abundantly.

Your physical life will one day end. Your real life is timeless spirit.

The birds and the flowers aren't worried or hurried. They know I'm taking care of them.

I'm taking care of you and everyone else too.

In step with me, the harmony within you is all around you too.

You're in my kingdom. You have everything you need.

Matthew 1:19 Matthew 4:1-11 Matthew 5 Matthew 6

Chapter 11 - Matthew Part 2

Live today as though it's the last day of your life on earth. For all you know, it could well be.

Be a conduit for my kindness and mercy.

Forget regrets and dismiss vain imaginings.

Be at peace in the present moment.

Don't worry about yesterday or tomorrow. Live a day at a time.

Accept others as you'd like to be accepted.

Why look at the minor faults in someone else when you have major faults of your own?

Who are you to criticize or advise?

Deal with your own faults first.

When you're perfect, then you'll be able to see clearly enough to look at someone else's faults and give them advice.

If a child asked you for bread, would you give them a stone? If you, with all your shortcomings, know how to give good things to a child, how much better do I know how to give good things to you.

Treat others the way you'd like to be treated. This sums up the Law and the Prophets.

Apply my teachings in your daily life. That gives you a firm foundation, like a house built on rock. When storms come, you're not shaken.

Be at peace. Your sins are forgiven.

You're one of those for whom I came. I welcome outcasts, sinners, the lonely and the lame. I bring freedom to those who are burdened with shame. I accept people as they are, in the midst of their pain. I heal with love, and you can do the same.

The new wine of a new consciousness can't be poured into the old wineskin of a former mindset. The old mindset can't contain it. If you try to pour the new wine into the old container, it will burst the old container and the new wine -- the new consciousness -- will be wasted. A new consciousness -- a new mind -- needs a new paradigm.

You've received freely. Give freely.

When you enter a place, give a peaceful greeting. If those in the place welcome you, your peace will also be with them. If they don't welcome you, your peace will remain with you.

If you're accused or maligned, don't defend yourself. Don't worry about what to say or how to say it. At the right time, if speaking is required, I'll give you the words to say. It won't be you speaking, but me speaking through you.

Matthew 6:34 Matthew 7 Matthew 9 Matthew 10:8-20

Chapter 12 - Matthew Part 3

There's nothing to worry about.

Every event is heaven-sent.

Not one sparrow falls to the ground without my knowledge and consent.

I'm watching over you too.

Lose your life and find your life in me.

Be conscious of I Who Am Within You. I refresh you.

Learn from me. I'm gentle and humble of heart. In me, you have peace.

The things you say reveal what's in your heart.

Sometimes, your words reveal a heart that's irritable. I'm transforming you. Increasingly, your words reveal a heart that's peaceful.

Forget yourself, take up your cross and follow me. Surrender your will -- completely. Align your will with mine. All that is and all that happens is part of my design.

If you'd like to enter my kingdom -- the kingdom of heaven -- then humble yourself and become like a little child. A little child is unselfconscious.

I'm in every person you come across during your earthly journey. Whatever you do for any one of them, you do for me.

I'm with you always.

Matthew 10:29-31   Matthew 10:39   Matthew 11:28-29

Matthew 12:34-36   Matthew 16:24-25   Matthew 18:3-4

Matthew 25:40 Matthew 28:20

Chapter 13 - Mark

You're my dearly loved child. I'm delighted with you.

Sometimes, after a spiritually uplifting experience, I bring you to the desert. You go from dancing on a cloud to sitting in the dirt. You discover new areas of sorrow and hurt.

In the desert, you feel perplexed and forsaken. It seems like the light you once had has been taken. You feel like you're wandering in the dark. Everything seems barren and stark.

You come out of the desert more humble than when you went in.

Be conscious of my presence, around you and within.

Your purpose is to be a means through which love flows to all.

In me you have a new life.

The more humble you are, the less often you think about yourself.

Offer up your will and your life to me, and trust in my love and mercy.

Forget yourself and follow me.

Humility sets you free.

Live with an attitude of holy indifference.

Faith transports you from the weird little world of your human understanding to the realm of Truth -- beyond space and time, and beyond any worldly paradigm.

Love others as you love yourself and, for their sake, make sure you love yourself.

Love yourself as I love you, and then love others that way too.

Mark 1:11-12 Mark 2:15-17 Mark 5:36-39 Mark 8:34-35
Mark 11:22-24 Mark 12:31

Chapter 14 - Luke Part 1

Mary glorifies me. She rejoices in me. She is the epitome of beauty, wisdom, love and humility.

I bring down the proud and lift up the humble.

I have mercy on all who turn to me.

Though Simeon told Mary that a sword would pierce her own soul too, she put her trust in me and saw my will in all that she went through.

Mary is your spiritual mother. She's the Star of the Sea. She's with you on your journey.

Go into the deep waters of your unconscious and let down the nets for a catch.

The healthy don't need a doctor, but the sick do. You have no reason to ever despair, because you can bring your damaged soul to me, the Divine Doctor, for repair.

The Home of Grace is always open and I am always there. It doesn't matter what condition you're in or what you've been through. Just knock, and the door will be opened to you.

Do good to those who hate you.

Bless those who curse you.

Pray for those who mistreat you.

If someone strikes you on one cheek, turn to them the other one also.

It's easy to love those who love you, but love your enemies too. Your reward will be great if you do. You'll be acting in accord with your true nature. You're one with me. I'm Love. I'm kind to the wicked and the ungrateful.

Be merciful, just as I'm merciful.

Don't judge and you won't be judged.

Don't condemn and you won't be condemned.

Forgive, and you'll be forgiven.

Luke 1:28-52 Luke 2:35 Luke 5:4 Luke 5:31 Luke 11:9
Luke 6:27-37

Chapter 15 - Luke Part 2

The measure you use will be measured to you.

How can you say to someone, 'Let me take the speck out of your eye,' when you don't realize that you have a plank in your own eye?

Take the plank out of your own eye first. Then you'll see clearly enough to take the speck from someone else's eye.

The more aware you are of my love for you, the more loving you are toward others.

Your sins have been forgiven, so move on. Why dwell on those sins anymore? They're gone.

Your trust in my love saves you. It delivers you from your sins and gives you a new life.

Go in absolute peace.

If someone acts in an unfriendly way, don't get upset. Just shake the dust off your feet and move on.

Don't look back. I've healed your past and set you free.

Live in my kingdom with gratitude and humility.

Why worry? Why hurry?

Walk slow, talk slow and think slow.

I know what I'm doing. I've been at it forever, beyond time.

Trusting in me gives you a peaceful mind.

Luke 6:38-42   Luke 7:47-50   Luke 9:5   Luke 9:62   Luke 12:22-31

Chapter 16 - Luke Part 3

Though you sometimes stray from what's right and true, you're still my child, no matter what you do.

As you trudge toward home with a repentant heart, I run out to greet you before you get to the gate. Embracing you, I say: Let's have a feast and celebrate! Let's have music and dancing. We'll invite everyone who's around. You were dead, but now you're alive! You were lost, but now you've been found!

I'm infinite.

I'm the essence of everything.

In me, you never lack anything.

Faith raises you beyond your fears.

Whatever is needed appears.

I guide and provide.

Whether you've indulged in riotous living, been self-righteous or unforgiving, my love heals and restores.

You're always with me, and all that I have is yours.

My kingdom is within you. It's a state of consciousness.

To enter into spiritual consciousness -- the kingdom of heaven -- be like a little child.

What is humanly impossible is possible for me.

Love people without attachment.

If you leave your home, spouse, siblings, parents or children for the sake of my kingdom, you'll have much more, both in your earthly life and in the life to come.

I seek and save whoever is lost.

Luke 15:11-24 Luke 15:31 Luke 17:21 Luke 18:9-14 Luke 18:16-17 Luke 18:27-30 Luke 19:10

Chapter 17 - John Part 1

In me, is life. My life within you is your light.

I am the true light that gives light to everyone.

You're my child.

You're not born of natural means. You're born of me.

From the fullness of my grace, you've received one blessing after another.

Grace and truth are revealed in Jesus Christ.

Your real self is Spirit.

Like the water and the wind, where you're going is where you are and have always been -- in union with me, the Infinite Eternal Essence within.

I didn't come into the world to condemn people, but to save them.

Trusting in me, you have eternal life and you won't be condemned. You've crossed over from death to life.

My Spirit gives life. The flesh doesn't count for anything.

Don't judge by appearances.

The world is real, but your perceptions of it are not real. They're only your perceptions.

Go beyond the realm of your senses. Go beyond what you think and feel. Look through the appearances and see the Real.

In me, you're free.

Listen to my voice within you and follow me.

In me, you have eternal life.

No one can take you from me.

You're one with me -- eternally.

John 1:4-17   John 3:8   John 3:17   John 5:24   John 6:63   John 7:24   John 8:36   John 10:27-29

Chapter 18 - John Part 2

I draw everyone to me.

I came into the world as a light to dispel the darkness.

In me, you live in the light.

Love others as I love you.

There's no need to be troubled about anything.

Trust in me.

Be where I am. I'm everywhere.

I'm the way, the truth and the life.

There's no way, truth or life apart from me. How could there be?

I'm Life Itself. I'm all, and I'm beyond all. I AM. I'm that which IS.

You can do the things that Jesus did and more, because I'm within you.

Anything you ask in my name is done.

Love enables you to obey my commands.

I'm within you.

Because I live, you live.

I'm your life. If I didn't live, you wouldn't live.

You're in me and I'm in you.

I teach you everything.

You have my peace. I've given it to you.

John 12:32 John 12:46 John 13:34 John 14

Chapter 19 - John Part 3

Apart from me you can do nothing, because apart from me you are nothing.

I'm the invisible substance of all that is.

I'm the immortal spirit of Life Itself, living in you, through you and as you, now and forever.

Love others as I love you.

I lead you into all truth.

You don't need a teacher or a guru. I show you how love makes everything new.

I turn your grief into joy.

In me you have peace.

In the world you'll have trouble, but don't worry. I Within
You have overcome the world.

This is eternal life: to know me.

All I have is yours and all you have is mine.

The full measure of my joy is within you.

You're not of the world, just as I'm not of the world.

You're one with me.

You have my glory.

I love you.

We're one. You, me, and everyone.

Be where I am and see my glory.

Look at everything through the lens of love.

Mary, your spiritual mother, is full of grace. Sometimes your heart's in a lonely place. You get lost in a jungle of appetites. You try to hide from all you fear. You lose your sense of direction and purpose and nothing seems clear. Mary comforts you in the confusion of darkness. She looks on you with compassion and mercy. She brings you to a place of serenity. She brings you to me.

John 15:5 John 15:12 John 16:13 John 16:20-22 John 16:33 John 17 John 19:27

Chapter 20 - Acts and Romans

There are many hardships in your earthly life. Every circumstance gives you an opportunity to transcend your self.

Your real self is one with me.

Unite your will with mine, and live in my kingdom -- beyond space and time.

In me you live and move and have your being.

I've poured out my love into your heart.

In union with me, you see goodness where you didn't see it before. Where sin abounds, grace abounds even more.

Your old self was crucified with Christ.

You don't understand what you do. What you want to do you don't do, and what you hate, you end up doing.

What you do are not the right things that you want to do; no, the wrong things that you don't want to do -- those you keep on doing.

You wonder why you keep messing up. You wonder why you seem so weak. You wonder why you fall so short of living the virtuous life that you seek. If you always acted virtuously, you'd no doubt feel self-satisfied -- and you could easily fall prey to spiritual pride.

There's no condemnation for you. I've set you free.

My spirit, the spirit that raised Jesus from the dead, is living in you.

Just like you, everyone else is my child too. So regard them as such.

I make everything work for your good.

Since I'm for you, does it matter who's against you? Since I justify you, does it matter who condemns you?

Nothing, below or above, can separate you from my love.

Don't conform any longer to the ways of the world.

I'm transforming you. I'm completely changing the way you think and how you view things.

Insofar as it depends on you, live at peace with everybody.

My kingdom is about trusting in me and living in peace and joy.

Accept others as I accept you. When you do that, you glorify me.

Acts 14:22 Acts 17:28 Romans 3:21-24 Romans 5:5-20
Romans 6:6 Romans 7:15-19 Romans 8 Romans 12:2
Romans 12:18 Romans 14:1 Romans 15:7

Chapter 21 - 1 Corinthians

Have not I made foolish the so-called wisdom of the world?

You have the mind of Christ.

My Spirit lives in you.

The so-called wisdom of this world is foolishness in my sight.

My judgement of you is the only one that matters.

Don't be concerned about how others judge you.

Don't even judge yourself.

You're one with me in spirit.

If you're a prophet or a mystic or a person with strong faith, but you don't have love, then you don't have anything.

If you have love, you have everything.

It's all about love.

I'm love and I'm within you.

Love is what I am and love is what I do.

Love others as I love you.

Love is patient and kind. It isn't envious, boastful or proud. It isn't rude, selfish or irritable. It doesn't keep a record of wrongs. It banishes fears. Love rejoices in the truth. It protects, trusts, hopes and perseveres.

Now you know only partially; later, you'll know fully, as fully as I know you.

By my grace, you are what you are.

Die daily.

Live as though you're already dead.

In humility, you're free.

Do everything in love.

1 Corinthians 1:20 1 Corinthians 2:16 1 Corinthians 3:16 1 Corinthians 3:19 1 Corinthians 4:3-4 1 Corinthians 6:17 1 Corinthians 13:2 1 Corinthians 13:4-7 1 Corinthians 13:12 1 Corinthians 15:10 1 Corinthians 15:31 1 Corinthians 16:14

Chapter 22 - 2 Corinthians

In suffering and sorrow, you're stripped of all that's frivolous.

I comfort you in all your troubles. You can then comfort others with the comfort you receive from me.

You share in the sufferings of Christ and through Christ you also receive comfort.

Disregard worldly views. Live according to my grace.

Your view of Reality is obscured by the veil of your limited mortal perspective. Therefore, you're not viewing Reality Itself. But in me, the veil is taken away.

Where my spirit is, there's freedom.

I'm transforming you into my likeness with ever-increasing glory.

Your worldly troubles are temporary, and they're achieving for you an eternal glory.

Keep your attention not on what's visible, but on what's invisible.

What's visible is only temporary. What's invisible is eternal.

Walk by faith, not by sight.

Let love rule you and guide you.

I'm the Immortal Reality of every person, including you. So why look at your self or anyone else from a worldly point of view?

Every person you see is a manifestation of me.

Look beyond the outer appearance. Look beyond what people say and do. Look beyond the disguise of the flesh. See them from a spiritual point of view.

Beyond time and beyond space -- that's the Truth behind each face.

In me, you're a new being. The old is gone. Everything's new.

You can be joyful even though you're experiencing an event that's sorrowful.

You can be sad, yet still be glad.

There are different types of sorrow. One is a worldly, self-centered type of sorrow. It leads to self pity and despair. The other is an inspired type of sorrow. It leads to holy things, such as deeper insights, a change of heart and salvation.

I bring you to a place that's beyond time and space.

In spiritual consciousness -- in the Garden of Eden -- you behold the daffodil of eternal life and the rose of infinite love, and, by my grace, you're born anew from above.

My grace is all you need.

My power works perfectly in your weakness.

Acknowledge that you're powerless.

Abandon yourself to me.

I do for you what you can't do for yourself.

Whether your struggles are with situations in the world, with inner turmoil or with sin, turn them over to me. I'll take care of everything.

2 Corinthians 1:3-5 2 Corinthians 1:12 2 Corinthians 3:16 -18   2 Corinthians 4:17-18   2 Corinthians 5:14-17   2 Corinthians 6:10 2 Corinthians 7:10 2 Corinthians 12:2-4 2 Corinthians 12:8-9

Chapter 23 - Galatians

You no longer live. I live -- in you.

I'm the One Life, appearing in many forms.

Everything's interconnected and united spiritually.

There's neither Jew nor Greek, male nor female. All are one in me.

I'm in your heart.

I've set you free, so live in freedom.

In me you have love, joy, peace, patience, kindness, goodness, faithfulness, gentleness and self-control.

Galatians 2:20   Galatians 3:28   Galatians 4:6   Galatians 5:1
Galatians 5:22-23

Chapter 24 - Ephesians

My mercy is so abundant, my love for you is so great, that while you were spiritually dead in disobedience, I brought you to life.

I've raised you up with Christ into the heavenly realms.

You've been saved by my grace through faith.

Your salvation isn't something you've earned by your own efforts, so you have no reason to feel proud or to boast. It's my gift.

I've made you what you are.

I've created you to do acts of kindness, which I've prepared in advance for you to do. I do them -- through you.

My spirit in your inner being gives you strength and power.

I dwell in your heart.

I lift you up out of your worldly delusions into the awareness of love.

In love, you're filled with my nature.

I do more than you can ask or imagine.

My power is always at work within you.

Be humble, gentle and patient.

In love, accept others as they are.

I'm within you and around you, permeating all and transcending all.

I'm in the air you breathe and in the food you eat.

I'm within everyone you meet.

I'm in the forest, the church building and the shopping mall.

I'm over all, through all and in all.

Put on your new self.

To put on your new self is to live out of the awareness of your real self.

Your real self is one with me.

When you bring the awareness of your new self to whatever you do, everything around you seems new too.

Be thoughtful and gracious when speaking.

Don't criticize, complain, gossip or boast.

Speak kindly about others.

Don't express your opinion or give advice unless you're asked to do so.

When you do express your opinion or give advice, do so with gentleness and humility.

Be tenderhearted and merciful.

Forgive others just as I have forgiven you.

You're my dearly-loved child.

My love flows through you to others.

Live as a child of light.

Make music in your heart and sing.

Be thankful for everything.

Ephesians 2:4-10   Ephesians 3:16-20   Ephesians 4:2-6

Ephesians 4:23-32   Ephesians 5:1-2   Ephesians 5:8

Ephesians 5:19-20

Chapter 25 - Philippians

I will complete the work that I've begun in you.

I'm working in you according to my good purpose.

Do everything without bickering or complaining.

You haven't yet been made perfect. That's okay.

I'm guiding you along the way.

Forget what's behind and keep heaven in mind.

You're a citizen of heaven.

You're on earth only for your allotted number of years. All people, things and events are the forms and ways through which my perfect will appears.   So be at peace -- even through the tears.

Be joyful!

Be gentle and considerate.

It's useless to worry about anything.

Trust me totally and be thankful for everything.

Leave everything to me, and my peace, which passes all understanding, will fill your heart and mind.

Keep your thoughts on things that are right, pure, lovely and true.

Whether you're praised or blamed, honored or shamed; be content.

Whether you're in sickness or in health, in poverty or in wealth; be content.

Whether you're in comfort or in pain, treated respectfully or with disdain; be content.

Be content in whatever situation you happen to be. I'm using it to bring you to me.

You can do all things through me. I give you strength.

Philippians 1:6   Philippians 2:13-14   Philippians 3:12-20
Philippians 4:4-13

Chapter 26 - Colossians

I've rescued you from the darkness and brought you into the kingdom of light.

When you first became aware of my unconditional love for you, you accepted it with trust and gratitude. Continue in that attitude.

Keep your mind on things above, not on things of this world.

You have died.

Your life is now in me.

I'm your real life.

I'm all and I'm in all.

Clothe yourself with compassion, kindness, gentleness, patience and humility. To those qualities, add love. It brings all of them together in perfect unity.

Forgive as I've forgiven you.

Let my peace rule in your heart. Let it guide you.

Trust in me and be thankful.

Be considerate in conversation.

Be thoughtful in answering a question.

Colossians 1:12-13   Colossians 2:6-7   Colossians 3:2-15
Colossians 4:6

Chapter 27 - 1 Thessalonians to Hebrews

Be joyful always.

Pray continually.

Give thanks in all circumstances.

I'm within you and around you, always and everywhere. Living in that awareness is living in continual prayer.

My will prevails whether you accept it serenely or rail against it, so why rail against it?

Whatever happens or doesn't happen is my will, and I will only what's best. Therefore, give thanks in all circumstances, because in all of them you're being blessed.

You can't be righteous on your own. You sin in how you think, speak and behave. The good news is -- you're one of those I came to save.

Everything I created is good. Nothing is to be rejected.

Receive everything with thanksgiving. Yes, everything.

My spirit fills you with power, love and peace.

Be peaceful, friendly and humble.

Don't presume that you know better than others what's best for them.

You're not responsible for the choices that others make.

People have the right to make their own decisions, even if they're making a mistake.

Each person has their own gifts and their own ways of doing things.

Each person is unique.

Though you might want to offer your opinion, avoid the temptation to speak.

Instead of meddling, let your faith increase.

Leave others to me and live in peace.

I don't condemn you. I don't kick you when you're down. I reach out my hand to help you off the ground.

Trust in my love. Approach the throne of grace with confidence.

Be kind to strangers, because it's the loving thing to do. Also, you never know -- they could be angels.

1 Thessalonians 5:16-18 1 Timothy 1:15 1 Timothy 4:4 2 Timothy 1:7 Titus 3:2 Hebrews 4:16 Hebrews 13:2

Chapter 28 - James

When you encounter various trials, big or small, be full of joy. They're opportunities to learn patience.

My will is expressed in the happenings of each moment.

Whatever is happening right now is what's best for you. So give thanks in all situations and be at peace.

Trusting in me is the essence of spiritual maturity.

Be quick to listen and slow to speak.

If you think you're spiritually enlightened and don't keep a tight rein on your tongue, you're kidding yourself, and your spirituality is worthless.

Let me guide you. I'll let you know whether you should speak or not. If it's better to be silent, I'll help you to be silent. If it's better to speak, I'll give you the right words to say.

Your earthly life is like a puff of smoke -- you appear for a little while and then you vanish.

Be patient -- with yourself and with every one.

Suffering is a mystery beyond what your mortal mind can comprehend. However, I'm with you in your suffering and it will end -- either in this life or when you begin the next.

Before long you won't have a physical body or a mortal mind. You'll have left them behind.

James 1:2-4   James 1:19   James 1:26   James 4:14   James 5:7-11

Chapter 29 - 1 Peter and 2 Peter

In me, you're holy.

You've been born again, not of what is temporary but of what is eternal.

If you're insulted, don't counter attack. If someone hurts you, don't think, 'I'll get them back.'

You don't have to settle scores or put other people 'in their place.' I deal with every one with a mysterious blend of justice and grace.

Through Christ, my glory has been revealed.

Be kind and humble.

If someone hurts you by what they say or do, don't retaliate. Just say, 'God bless you,' and you'll be blessed too.

Show love to others. Love covers a lot of sins.

Turn everything over to me.

I've given you everything you need for life and holiness.

You share in my divine nature, and by that nature, you overcome the corruption of the world.

Time and eternity are mysteries beyond what you can grasp or convey.

In me, a day is like a thousand years and a thousand years are like a day.

1 Peter 1:15   1 Peter 1:23   1 Peter 2:23-24   1 Peter 3:8-9   1 Peter 4:8   1 Peter 5:7   2 Peter 1:3-4   2 Peter 3:8

Chapter 30 - 1 John and 2 John

Confess your sins to me and trust in my mercy.

I make you holy.

Try to avoid sin. However, if you do sin, know that you have one who speaks to me in your defense—Jesus Christ, the Righteous One.

Loving others, you live in the light.

Your sins have been forgiven because of Christ.

You're my beloved child. That's what you are!

Love others. Love comes from me.

In Love, you've been born of me and you know me.

You live in me and I live in you.

You are, in essence, a spiritual being living in a spiritual Reality.

I am love.

In love, you live in me and I live in you.

There's no fear in love.

Love makes fear disappear.

You show your love for me by loving others.

You have eternal life in me.

Live a life of love.

1 John 1:9   1 John 2:1   1 John 2:10-12   1 John 3:1   1 John 4:7-21   1 John 5:11   2 John 1:6

Amen.

Thank you for reading From God to You.

If you'd like to say hello or send a comment or a question, I'd be glad to hear from you.   My email address is: sjcurran100@hotmail.com.

Thanks again.

Made in the USA
Charleston, SC
08 March 2014